The Stream of Life

Poems Reflecting the Flow of Life

Gilbert A. Franke

Red Flannel Quilt Publishing
130 N Harris St
Bellville TX 77418

Copyright © 2011 Gilbert A. Franke

All rights reserved.

ISBN: 0615538274
ISBN-13: 978-0615538273

DEDICATION

To Beth,
the occasion and inspiration for many of these poems,
the constant companion in even more,
and the patient audience of them all,
my thanks and my love!

CONTENTS

Preface	vii
Headwaters	1
Pond	9
Brook	19
Lake	27
River	37
Delta	49
Bay	59
Index	69

Preface

The Flowing Stream of Life

As darkening clouds oppress the summer sky
With subtle monotones of autumn's art,
I slowly start my steps to say good-bye;
My heavy feet are lighter than my heart,
And yet they drag, reluctant, to the call
Of circumstance beyond a puny will.
My every nerve employed to break the fall
Cannot prevent a bloody, lingering kill
As soul is torn from soul in silent strife.
Not knowing when we'll meet again, or where,
I'm standing in the flowing stream of life
Afraid to choose my path and take a dare.
    What will I do? Be led by fate, or fight?
    Preserve my love, or let it fade from sight?

Like a mountain hiker who has decided to follow a tumbling stream, we have to make decisions at crucial junctions in life without all the evidence in hand. The impact of our choices is affected by where we are. In the headwaters we may pick our way with delight. In swifter currents missteps are dangerous. Heavy burdens become liabilities. Sometimes the movement is imperceptible, allowing time for deep reflection and soul-searching. As we near the end of our journey, we might meander and lose our way. Eventually like stream water that reaches the bay, we find ourselves at our journey's end.

    These poems have been selected to reflect passage along the stream of life. Some connections will be readily apparent. Others might be lost in backwater eddy currents! The reader will find his or her own applications.

HEADWATERS

What can you tell of the currents below
when you stand in the cool mountain heights?
Here's where the spring from the melt of the snow
births a stream in the clear, summer nights.

The Stocking Cap

In the corner of a trunk I found it,
cradled up beside the family Bible
    where you kept the names and dates
    that told you who you were
        long after you forgot just what they meant.

    An old, blue, stocking cap!

The same warm feeling covered me
as on that day you pulled it down upon my head
    and took me from the children's home,
    the newest member of your family.

And now, because you are not there,
I keep it by the window where you used to sit,
    to tell me who I am,
    and to remind me who I was
        before you found me.

The Ranch

On the Fourth of July we would all gather there;
There were uncles and aunts and my cousins so fair.
We would run; we would romp! We had room there to roam;
We had glorious fun at my grandparents' home!
And on Thanksgiving Day all the relatives came,
For my grandmother's meals were well known in their fame,
There was Christmas with carols around the tall tree.
All these mem'ries, I'm sure, will be cherished by me.
We would climb up so high in the old cedar tree
That we thought we could fly, oh so far, fast, and free!
There were nuts we could gather that lay on the ground,
While the leaves would fall swirling around and around.
In the shade of the orchard we loved to go play;
There was baseball and swinging to fill up the day.
There were picnics with melons we ate in the shade.
We would play on the slide and on roads that we made
In the sand with a hoe. And we loved to sneak down
To the cellar so cool, with its mystery around.
    Oh yes! This is The Ranch that I knew with delight,
    And these are the memories I dream of at night!

The Fireworks

On the Fourth of July we would gather for fun
In a family tradition that must have begun
In the year our Aunt Gertrude was born — 1910,
Three days after the national birthday had been;
And although we know now that the sparklers those nights
Were to celebrate liberty, freedom, and rights,
I'll bet most of my cousins back then would concur
That the fireworks had really been set off for her!
For in so many ways Aunty Gertrude, you see,
Had declared independence and set herself free
From her chair and her room and the confines of home.
It has often been said we can easily roam
Through the centuries and travel to far away lands
Just by moving through books that we hold in our hands.
That is just what she did! And she took us along
In the rhyme of a poem or tune of a song
On those hot summer days with her feet on the bed
As she told us the stories she'd heard of or read.
    Aunty Gertrude encouraged our minds to be free,
    And that's why her fireworks declare liberty!

True Remedies from Home

A lot of things I often use today
when colds and pains and heartaches trouble me
are remedies that worked to chase away
those ailments when my mother doctored me.
I must admit I liked the peach tree leaf
tea better than the peach tree switch! And yet
I didn't like that tea too much! --- Relief
for stuffy heads and scratchy throats we'd get
with hoar-hound candy Mother cooked from weeds
that grew out in the woods! Or tea she'd boil
with lemon juice and honey. --- Other needs
were cured with orange juice and castor oil!
    One remedy still works to heal me of
    my hurts and pains today – my mother's love!

To Grandmother's House

"It's over the river and through the woods,"
    or that's what we used to say,
But over the interstate, through the 'hoods
    is how we all go today!

We can't make the trip with a horse and sleigh;
    the journey would be too far.
We down-load a 'mapquest' to show the way,
    and load up our truck or car.

With twinkling eyes and a greeting said,
    there's Grandmother at the door.
The smell of fresh coffee and home-made bread
    gives promise of so much more.

We sit and we talk as we watch the birds
    that come to the window sill.
They pay no attention to all our words,
    but tend to their feeding still.

Out there in the yard is a shady tree
    where children can climb and play.
With family around you can plainly see
    how Grammer enjoys this day!

The Roots and the Branches

Your sorrows, your heartaches, your angers, your joys,
The games of your sister, and your brother's toys,
Your family, your school, your home, and your friends,
Your parents' religion on which yours depends,
That's the environment you had as a child;
That is what makes you pugnacious or mild,
And the roots that grow deep in your knowledge and lore
Shall send up a trunk that toward heaven will soar.
You are that trunk, and your stature depends
On the goals of your life, your ambitions and ends.
If your roots grow too shallow, and if they're not strong,
Then your trunk will be gnarled, your future go wrong;
If the feeders that nourish, are powerful enough
To conquer discord and smooth out the rough,
Then your tree can grow sturdy and straight;
You may be a Schweitzer or Dooley come late.
Out of your life will grow branches of love
Sturdy and spreading, and way up above
The sorrow and sickness so common in life.
Your leaves will embrace mankind in his strife,
And, being examples, they'll point out the way
For your brothers to follow until that great day
When they too can attain a magnificent spread
From the roots that hold fast in their nourishing bed.

POND

*Trickles of water meander across
a wide meadow of sweet, alpine hay.
Pooling below, it drops silt from the dross
as it gathers more strength for the way.*

A Vision Idealized

I saw her once when August sun shone bright;
She had a flight of fairies in her hair.
I kept a watch; she never came back there.
I saw her in the evening's fading light;
I thought she was a vision to my sight,
But in my dreams she never was so fair!
I wished to call to her, but did not dare
For fear that startled, she would run in fright.
May scheming Cupid shoot a fiery dart
To kindle love that lasts as long as life --
A soul-felt love of diamond quality;
And may a fiber grow from heart to heart
So strong that neither discord, time, nor strife
Can separate her or her love from me.

Like Threads of a Spider

Our lives like threads of a spider meet
As we tread life's road with weary feet.
We cannot say where the web will cross.
In such a way we are at a loss
When we think of friends that have come and gone
And the many more in our lives anon.

Those friends who loved in days of yore
May never see each other more,
For the pathways of their lives may part
With many an ache to the rending heart.
But who can say? We can't be sure
That the friends won't meet if their hearts endure.

As one green spruce stands on a hill
With its friends all gone and the landscape still,
There is the future scene where friends abound,
Those left behind in the dear home ground,
Left behind when the spruce was moved,
True to the spruce, as their trials proved.

When a cod is taken from the sea
How sad both it and the others must be.
But the cod may find a former chum
Who to the fish boat may have come.
Whatever the future may hold for the cod,
You may be sure it is guided by God.

Wherever we go and whatever we do
We must trust by our faith in our Savior, too;
Hold fast to the doctrine as you have been taught;
Let nothing shake your faith for ought,
The things that you see and hear and learn
Must take second place to your spirit's concern.

Our lives are led by God's own hand,
And friends are made at His command.
Let us trust in Him that His Will will be
Of the greatest good for you and me.
That whatever His plan for our futures may hold,
He will shape our lives in His merciful mold.

Something Made of Bronze

The drops were clinging to the leaves as long
As they would dare, then dropping moistly down.
Some hit against the glass as if to drown
Her from my sight -- but like a haunting song
She clung between white curtains just as strong
As to the shadows of my mind: her crown
Of golden hair, her soft pink lips and gown,
Her face, struck dumb by some inhuman wrong.
I turned and walked into the future then,
Content to leave her gently in the past.
I left, but still I see her standing there
Within her rain streaked-glass and curtain pen.
Her image, pressed upon my mind, is cast
Like something made of bronze -- but with more care.

A Teardrop

A teardrop fell from her eyelid
    As a pearl from an oyster shell,
For she feared that her love would be wasted;
    But only time could tell.

As the days marched by in their order
    Like sentries on a castle wall,
Her love grew fuller and stronger;
    But she feared his heart would fall.

It was years 'til they could be married;
    Their love had begun too soon,
For it grew too fast toward a climax
    In the pale, wan light of the moon.

Had fate tempered their longing with patience,
    Or let them love at a riper age,
They might have fulfilled their wishes
    And turned the wedding page.

A teardrop fell from her eyelid
    As she sat on a lonely dune
Where once they both had cuddled,
    Who loved too well and too soon.

A Paper Cannot Hold

While camera, walls, and people coldly stare,
Our foolish hero smiles just warm enough,
And lights awake to heat the golden air;
The eye of glass gives out a chilling puff,
And in a trite his silly, frozen face
Is slapped upon the paper, still as death.
Now slowly, with your finger, you may trace
The shadows of his lips, but still no breath
Will touch it, though you wait a hundred years.
No eyes will close at night when you're asleep;
Nor will that empty smile give way to tears,
Though many pains may cause your heart to weep.
  A paper cannot hold the love that gives
  My heart to you, and with you, darling, lives.

Waiting

We're living a life full of waiting.
We wait for a letter today.
We wait for a phone call this weekend.
We wait for the weekend to stay.
We wait for a summer of frolic.
We wait for a time yet to come.
We wait for that time with a yearning
that makes what we wait for more fun.

The Season's Over

My head is cold; the wintry wind
Howls fiercely through my brain.
It freezes thought; it numbs the mind;
There's snow and sleet and rain.

Then thought of you, like spring's first beams
Melts all my icy grief.
And here or there, a bud, it seems,
Springs up beside a leaf.

The flowers bloom and birdies sing.
They hop from twig to twig,
But I can't fly to you on wing;
The distance is too big.

The shortest way from heart to heart
Is not a simple line.
Although our homes are far apart,
Your heart is close to mine.

BROOK

*Swiftly the course down the rocky ravine
gains direction and purpose and force,
shouting with joy in this turbulent scene
as it joins a new, cascading source!*

Pals

Out on the prairie near Chatfield
a young, German Mädchen grew up.
She plowed with a mule in the rich, fertile field
and cooked tasty meals served on platter and cup.

Out of the brush south of Blewett
a lanky, young cowboy rode tall.
He sang with vaqueros when campfires were lit
while rounding up doggies to ship in the fall.

Families would gather for worship,
and many would visit all day.
He played his guitar and sang songs that he wrote.
In letters she shared what their horses would say.
    She was his comfort and bastion;
    He was her trustworthy pal.

Then came the time they would treasure;
they trusted each other for life,
committing their future and love to God's care,
affirming each other as husband and wife.
    He was her courage and champion;
    She was his soul mate and pal.

Carving a life from the land at
a time when the living was tough,
they modeled the love of the Lord in their home.
With little to spare they had more than enough.
    They were each other's companions;
    Each was a true, faithful pal.

What Love Is

The golden sun arose to meet the day,
And from the east he blinked a misty eye;
The morning's breezes quickly swept away
The specks of star-dust from the August sky.
It didn't seem like summer, not at all;
The birds were fooled, the weather was so fair.
It should have been a day in spring or fall;
There simply was that feeling in the air.
My thoughts were happy, and my mind was light
As all creation joined my heart-felt song.
Some people call this feeling love, alright;
But I would say that they are partly wrong.
It may be this, but it is much more too;
For now I know that love is really you!

Dedication: Sonnets From the Portuguese

The gems embodied in these works of art
Are veiled in diction strange; may every thought --
Implied, expressed -- through careful reading sought,
Spring forth a sparkling jewel inside your heart,
And to your spirit, my beloved, impart
A wealth of riches never to be bought.
Then, when you've read them several times, they ought
To grow within your soul, a counterpart
In empathy to what will grow in mine.
A bond of kindred feelings will be ours
Which draws its source along the plotted line
of "Sonnets From the Portuguese," and towers
Above the common loves, a stately pine,
Its roots in Browning's plane, in heaven its bowers.

The Rose Buds

A tiny shoot was nurtured by the hand
Of some unknown, unknowing man who felt
The urge to place a rose branch in the sand.
It grew, as winter's sun began to melt
And move the frozen juice of life which filled
The stalk. It forced a root to gingerly
Explore the warm, moist crystals there. That thrilled
The plant and caused some fresh activity
Above the ground. It grew a leaf at first;
And then a larger twig appeared to hold
A host of leaves and thorns. At last it burst
The soft, green bark with three small buds of gold!
    These fragile buds perform a task divine,
    Becoming tributes to my Valentine.

Thoughts on Our Engagement

If only then we could have known
what pains and sorrows we would know,
would I have dared to ask at all,
and you so quickly give consent
to be the mother of our sons?

One devastating loss
still festers in our soul;
and years of healing pain
still work to make another whole.

I would not have you bear
these burdens once again,
but glad I am that you
are here with me to share the pain.

And this, my dear, I say for sure,
if I had known what joys
and pleasure we should know,
my quest had made a spill
of breakfast milk seem slow –
while waiting for your quick reply
had seemed like watching children grow!

Their very precious childhood days
still living in our minds
are treasured bonus joys
enriching us so many ways.

LAKE

*Here the brook calms from its rapid descent
as the waters lie peaceful and still.
Evening light, fading, gives hasty consent
and reflects both the forest and hill.*

The Prophet
*(dedication of Kahil Gibran's
'The Prophet' as a gift)*

No prophet tells the changeless law of fate
Or spreads a doom required to come to pass.
The honest prophet's ringing tones of brass
Are not metallic, cold, and heartless hate.
Instead, he speaks before the hour is late,
Of fragrant blossoms, hope, and verdant grass
To make a liar of his prophet's glass
And turn the heedful to a better state.
A poet-prophet of the soul who speaks
In vague and misty terms of pleasure's pain,
Of joyous sorrow, slaves of freedom, life --
Is one who points to love, and in it seeks
To show the wary spirit what to gain
And how to reach a vict'ry through his strife.

The Forerunner
*(dedication of Kahil Gibran's
'The Forerunner' as a gift)*

The faithful herald runs before the king
Announcing splendor, pomp, and majesty.
He calls the people from their shops to see
The royal carriage, and to loudly sing
The glories of their sovereign. Many bring
Him honor, paying homage on their knee;
But he must follow in his heraldry
Or else there are no hamlet bells to ring.
The spirit-herald of our life goes out --
A forerunner to what our life will be.
'Tis he who calls our reason to its needs
And stirs emotion to a rousing shout
That welcomes life in all its majesty --
A life, which follows where the herald leads.

The Madman
(dedication of Kahil Gibran's
'The Madman' as a gift)

What cause have I to play a madman's fool
When all the world is doped with sanity?
Behind their seven masks, they cannot see --
Like poor Laocoon's attempt to rule
The serpents -- powers that grapple me in cruel
Death-dealing grip. Then why should I agree
To veil my thoughts in cloaks like theirs and be
Another sane man in a stagnant pool?
If I must fain affected passion's tears,
And answer "yes" when all I feel is "no";
If this is how the sane man acts, then I
Shall be a madman! Sanity appears
To father falsehood, lies, deceit -- and so
It steals life from the self and lets it die.

Grace

The god of land and sky had carried out
A parched earth policy on us that year.
The crops dried up, and I began to doubt
That it would ever rain. I hid my fear
Of famine as I loudly cursed the wide
Expanse of vacant space above my fields
Where dark, black, noisy clouds should hide
The light of day. I thought, "A god who wields
Such power should make us suffer for some sin
Or he must take the blame in every case!
I won't admit to hideous crimes and pin
The guilt on me! Is this your god of grace?!"
    Time passed; rain fell; crops grew; then I recalled
    With shame my accusations of the Lord.

A New Year's Fig

A golden-brown and juicy fig, it lay
secure beside its sister, quite content
to rest there in the basket through the day
and soak the warmth and comfort others lent.
One day to his dismay he saw a hand
that sorted through the basket choosing figs
to eat. A dreadful fate for him to land
upon a salad plate! Behind some twigs
he hid to flee the dangers of that hour! --
He learned this secret there behind that wood:
a fig that will not give itself must sour
to feed the soil before God calls it good.
    A child of God can soak up love from those
    around, but when he learns to give, he grows.

Cries of Agony

A nameless fear assails my soul, and strife
constricts my aching heart. I see my sons
and daughters go to war against the ones
who wield the blade of terror's deadly knife.
These are my flesh and blood, my very life!
My dress is colored blue from smoking guns
and red that splatters on the hills and runs
into the endless shadows of the night.
Beyond the dark horizon, clouds of white
explosions are emblazoned on my eye.
My children sacrifice their lives for me
despite my cries of agony. Well might
resolve of will be lost and courage die.
I know, for I am Lady Liberty!

The Pilgrim Servant

O Pilgrim Servant, when God calls to send
you from your home to ventures without end,
and you step out with confidence in God
to go where none have been, by paths untrod,
you will not face your greatest fears alone,
for God will guide through perils still unknown.
    God bless you on your servant way and hold
    you in His hand, that you may be so bold!
Supported through God's love, your every groan
bears on its breath your prayers to heaven's throne.
He leads you by His hand and Shepherd's rod
and sends you forth to share the love of God.
To places you don't know, our God will tend
your footsteps safely to your journey's end.

Thursday Group

We gather as friends, yet more than friends, around
good coffee, pastries, study of the Word.
We bring the heartaches and the joys we've found
among God's people, things we've seen and heard,
your greatest joy, my most disturbing pain,
and things that seem no consequence at all.
When pretense falls, confession's greatest gain
is comfort, strength, and courage in our Call.
Bound by the grace of Christ, we share a task:
together, mining from the Word of God,
we learn to share eternal gems that last,
to bear the duty of the Shepherd's rod.
    A cry, a laugh, a prayer, the Gospel's fruit –
    these are the minutes of our Thursday Group!

RIVER

*Channeled in banks that have widened with time
where the water runs steady and deep,
currents continue their gentle decline
with eternal appointments to keep.*

Golden Spires
(upon seeing a rainbow over the cathedral in Magdeburg, Germany)

Golden spires
in a sunset wash
stand beneath
a million prisms'
fractured light
extending pointed praise
    in Magdeburg.

Their witness
of five hundred years
stands dull and
insignificant
in contrast to
the brilliant colors of
    God's covenant.

Windows in the Sky

O Lord, I'm not complaining!
    I know we prayed for weeks
        without an end,
    and prayers are surely answered
        in Your time.

Now when my old computer
      won't respond
      although I click an icon
        several times,
I start to comprehend
      when there upon the screen
      one application opens
        up three times!

Lord, can't you sort of shut those
      windows down,
because the land is flooding
    and still it keeps on raining
        all the time!

The Wind Blows On

A thousand warriors on a rocky ridge
watch over countless miles of desert sage.
They slash the air with triple bladed swords
and slice the dusty wind in spiral coils.
Stripping power from this attacking foe,
they bundle up the precious spoil of war
and send it off in multi-megawatts
on networked trails of shiny filaments
to power the plants and homes across the land.
The wind, undaunted by the fray, blows on.

Juggling Griefs

Look at him, poor wretched man
juggling griefs from hand to hand
never letting any fall
just like some magician's ball!

Holding grudges close to chest
thinks he knows reprisal best
always seeking eye for eye
gives his oath to justify!

If some court would rule for him
each injustice to condemn
still he would not find a peace
could not let his grieving cease.

Finally one more sad despair
adds a burden he can't bear
'til the sorry, spinning lot
all come crashing down on top.

Getting Free

Look at that vindictive man
struggling out as best he can,
but he cannot quite break free
from his own recriminy.

Pushing, pulling grief from shame
still he's trapped there all the same
underneath that messy pile
blaming others all the while.

If he sought a righteous rule
he would surely play the fool
for his grievances are less
than he himself has to confess.

Only One can set him free
from these burdens' tyranny
rescued by the Father's grace
in the Savior's loving face.

Some Old Resolves

I dusted off some old resolves
    to start this brand new year.
I'm really not concerned too much;
    they're hardly worn at all!

I'll neither judge another's heart
    nor tell the tales I hear.
I'll live the kind of life I ought
    so I can stand up tall.
I'll eat and drink a little less
    and walk a whole lot more.
I'll spend more time in solitude,
    in worship and in prayer.
My family will take center stage.
    I'll really help the poor.
And I will treat the little ones
    with greater love and care.

It doesn't take me very long
    to recognize my fate;
Year after year these broken goals
    reveal a sorry trace.
Resolve of mind is not enough
    to rectify my state:
The very best that I can do
    is live by God's good grace.

Crofting Inn

(for Scott and Gail McCoy, owners,
'Crofting Inn B and B, Cloudcroft, NM)

Up here on the mountain tops
the high clouds come crofting in,
up here where the worry stops
and our hearts' new hopes begin.

The weary who need some rest
for a hundred years or more
have found that this place is best
to renew and to restore.

Now this is the place to be
when your sins oppress your soul,
so follow along with me
and meet the One who can make you whole.

Big, Black Grackle

Big, black grackle with a yellow eye
walking like a pharaoh, your head held high!
What are you thinking as you cross my lawn,
looking for your breakfast in the early dawn?

Big, black grackle with a prideful air
watching for a hopper with your hungry stare!
What are you finding in my carpet grass,
catching bugs and crickets in your beak's strong grasp?

Big, black grackle with your jaunty steps
wanting to impress me with your confidence!
I know what you are doing with your raucous call –
trying to make me think that you're not scared at all!

A Gathering of Peers

Blank faces stare from rows of citizens
    seated in this weekly lottery
    waiting to win a place on a jury panel.

An occasional smile breaks somber features
    as another's name is called.

Each face hides apprehension,
    tolerance,
    resentment,
    and annoyance;
betraying a superior smugness,
    knowing that this pool
    couldn't possibly be
    a gathering of my peers!

DELTA

*So many paths in the wetlands, that lead
through a labyrinth placed in their way,
wind around islands of cattail and reed
while they search for the mouth of the bay.*

Fill Your Calendar!

It dawned on me one day: in vain
I looked both far and near;
Beyond the middle of the month
my calendar was clear!
I didn't have a thing to do;
I wondered if my life was through!
But now I have this calendar,
and I have written in,
From day to day, and every day
I live for serving Him.

FAITH TRACKS - 1

*(For Marcia, on her new venture
with Christus Spohn)*

Somewhere beyond the wardrobe door
the word of grace rang clear,
and stepping out of Narnia
you followed God's call here.

Along the way you found the one
to make your life complete,
but in a sudden, wrenching twist
death knocked you off your feet.

With many steps through lonely lands
you traced your troubled way,
providing comfort, hope and joy
much more than you could say.

You left your home and motherland
and journeyed here to stay;
while those you blessed, the Lord has blessed
and sped you on your way.

FAITH TRACKS - 2

*(For Marcia, on her new venture
with Christus Spohn)*

              Not knowing
how or where or when,
nor to what mortal end
your life was flowing,
              yet setting
out with confidence
that God alone made sense,
and humbly letting
              the Spirit
lead you on the way
by what God had to say
when you could hear it,
              now, nearly
stumbling, you look back
and see the winding track
of faith more clearly.

Sparrow in the Snow

Little sparrow in the snow,
won't you come to harm?
Is there something I don't know?
How can you be warm?
Find a snowdrift; turn about;
duck your head down low!
Fluff your feathers; spread them out;
burrow in the snow!

Even when the cold wind blows
cutting like a knife,
God who made you surely knows
what you need for life,
in his mercy shelters you,
watches constantly,
loves his other creatures, too,
and will rescue me.

Out the Window at the Farm

Watch my grandma stooped and low
slowly to the window go.
See her shining light brown eyes
and the cardinal she spies.
Then she spots another bird:
"There's that mocker that I heard!
Sometimes at the break of day
little turkeys come this way.
And a cautious speckled fawn
seeks its mother through the dawn."

– – –

"Glad you came to sit by me
all these living things to see
out the window at the farm
once the weather starts to warm."

Words Unspoken
(For Frances)

I watch you move across the room and
    thrill to hear you softly call my name.
You come to me and take my hand and
    once again confess your love to me.
You surely know I love you, too!
There's never been a time that I have failed
    to meet your longing eyes with mine!

I feel your warm lips on my cheek and
    turn my head just slightly to your kiss.
Now, as you stand here by my bed
    I see the silent tears well in your eyes.
I know you love me still, my dear!
I only wish these words, unspoken yet,
    could form upon my stricken tongue.

Consider the Source

Bent back . . .
        Stark spine . . .
                Bold bones . . .

I rub her aching back
    with analgesic cream;
I feel the crumbling calcium
    of her vertebrae;
I see the labored breathing
    of her shrunken sides.

Considering the source of my life,
    I give thanks for my mother!

BAY

*Gently the current flows into the sea,
now embraced by the flood of the deep;
caught in the body, from hurry set free,
it will rest in an ocean of sleep.*

A Telling Loss

In casual conversation
    with a friend I hadn't seen in years,
    I asked, "How's Harry?"
With a touch of anger
    as if he'd left her holding
    a preemptive bid
    for the winning rubber
    in last week's game of bridge,
    she brought me up to date:
        "He passed!" she said.

In Memory of Alex

My little child, today my heart is torn!
So many plans and dreams already lay
Before you in my thoughts when you were born!
Those hopes would never know the light of day.
As glistening droplets fell upon your breast,
And God spoke words of promise to your soul,
The grace of Christ too quickly gave you rest
From your short struggle in this sinful world!
But even if for just a moment's span
Your little lungs inhaled the breath of life,
I thank the Lord, I took you in my hand
To touch with water and the Spirit's Life.
    You are a gift from God, so willingly
    We give you back to Him who set you free.

Like a Good Book

When I finish a good book and lay it to rest,
vivid thoughts of the hero still race through my mind.
I review all the drama, the good and the best;
and then sometimes I read it more slowly to find
every smile and expression each character wore.
I return to adventures I'd like to recall
or a dormant emotion I want to explore.

But with life there's no way to find answers at all
when the last page is turned and the hero is gone.
So I treasure the past, and I try to pretend
that I knew the cast well while the pageant went on,
for their memories are all that we have in the end.

I still wonder sometimes at the path our life took
as I dwell on the chapters I thought were the best,
how we stepped from the page at the end of the book
when the hero we loved was so soon laid to rest.

Dachau – April 29, 1945

I cried that day, like never before
    though I thought I'd never cry again.
I cried that day, as I grieved
    for years irrecoverable,
    and hopes unfulfilled,
    for hatred inexpressible,
        vengeance unrequited,
        suffering unexplainable.
I cried that day for joy
    when American troops
    came through the gates.
I cried that day
    for friends who died the day before
        and others, an eternity ago.

Crosses by the Side of the Road

They used to be items of mere curiosity,
Peaking some interest and waking my sympathy
For family members and dear, loving friends
Of those who had met with swift, untimely ends
At spots that are burdened with grief-filled loads
And are marked now with crosses beside many roads.

But now I can tell you where every one stands
Around the country and throughout the lands
Where I drive to and from on my weekly go-rounds:
Two by the railroad on neatly mowed grounds;
One at the light that is north of our town;
Two more by a storm ditch where two people drowned.

They show up at strange, unpredictable places,
And every one leaves small, indelible traces
Of sorrow, a bitter-sweet memory of pain,
On this super-highway, down that country lane.
Each cross by the side of the road, every one,
Has become a memorial mark for my son.

The Old Honda
(In memory of Norman Johnson)

There in the shed his old Honda still stands,
sporting a mantle of rust,
resting at ease from the highways' demands,
gathering a covering of dust.

It has been long since the thrill of the road
called him to places remote,
years since the saddle seat carried a load
more than his black leather coat.

Patiently waiting, his faithful dog sits
under these blue Texas skies,
keeping a vigil that he never quits,
watching with far-away eyes.

Never again will they follow the quests
that once together they'd seek,
now that forever his memory rests
on the banks of that old Hick'ry Creek.

Today He Would be Thirty-Five
(To Ethan on January 10, 2011)

Today he would be thirty-five,
your younger sibling, if alive.

While sorting through a packing box
we found his trophies: coins and rocks,
some patches earned, 4-H and Scout,
(We couldn't bear to throw them out.)
a bunch of pipes and humidor,
a dried corsage, and something more –
a tempting liquid in a flask!
Then we recalled the Pyrex glass
condenser borrowed from the lab,
the old grape wine that tasted bad,
his brandy wine experiment,
the fun he had distilling it!

We thought we ought to drink a toast,
your mom and I; we did almost,
but what we really want to do
is share this special bond with you.

We pause and raise our glasses now,
reflecting, and consider how
our lives are tempered where they touch.
This timely drink can't mean as much
to anyone who'll ever be
in all the world, but just us three.

INDEX

A Gathering of Peers	47
A New Year's Fig	33
A Paper Cannot Hold	16
A Teardrop	15
A Telling Loss	61
A Vision Idealized	11
Big, Black Grackle	46
Consider the Source	57
Cries of Agony	34
Crofting Inn	45
Crosses by the Side of the Road	65
Dachau – April 29, 1945	64
Dedication: Sonnets from the Portuguese	23
Faith Tracks - 1	52
Faith Tracks – 2	53
Fill Your Calendar	51
Getting Free	43
Golden Spires	39
Grace	32
In Memory of Alex	62
Juggling Griefs	42
Like a Good Book	63
Like Threads of a Spider	12
Out the Window at the Farm	55
Pals	21
Some Old Resolves	44
Something Made of Bronze	14
Sparrow in the Snow	54

INDEX

The Fireworks	5
The Flowing Stream of Life	vii
The Forerunner	30
The Madman	31
The Old Honda	66
The Pilgrim Servant	35
The Prophet	29
The Ranch	4
The Roots and the Branches	8
The Rose Buds	24
The Season's Over	18
The Stocking Cap	3
The Wind Blows On	41
Thoughts on Our Engagement	25
Thursday Group	36
Today He Would be Thirty-Five	67
To Grandmother's House	7
True Remedies from Home	6
Waiting	17
What Love Is	22
Windows in the Sky	40
Words Unspoken	56

www.ingramcontent.com/pod-product-compliance
Lightning Source LLC
Chambersburg PA
CBHW061506040426
42450CB00008B/1506